I0165626

Invisible Land of Love

Invisible Land of Love

Poems of Chonggi Mah

Translated by Youngshil Cho

Homa & Sekey Books
Paramus, New Jersey

FIRST EDITION

The book was originally published in Korean in 1980, by Moonji Press, Seoul, Korea.
Copyright © 2022 by Chonggi Mah
English Translation Copyright © 2022 by Youngshil Cho

This book is published with the support of the Literature Translation Institute of Korea (LTI Korea).

All rights reserved. No part of this book may be reproduced, stored in a retrieval system, or transmitted in any form, or by any means, electronic, mechanical, photocopying, recording or otherwise, without prior permission from the publisher.

Library of Congress Cataloging-in-Publication Data
Names: Ma, Chong-gi, 1939- author. | Cho, Yŏng-sil, translator.
Title: Invisible land of love / poems of Chonggi Mah ; translated by
   Youngshil Cho.
Other titles: An poinŭn sarang ŭi nara. English
Description: First edition. | Paramus, New Jersey : Homa & Sekey Books,
   [2022]
Identifiers: LCCN 2021048353 | ISBN 9781622461035 (paperback)
Subjects: LCSH: Ma, Chong-gi, 1939---Translations into English. | LCGFT:
Poetry.
Classification: LCC PL992.49.C4 A8413 2022 | DDC
   895.71/4--dc23/eng/20211206
LC record available at https://lccn.loc.gov/2021048353

Published by Homa & Sekey Books
3rd Floor, North Tower
Mack-Cali Center III
140 E. Ridgewood Ave.
Paramus, NJ 07652
Tel: 201-261-8810, 800-870-HOMA
Fax: 201-261-8890
Email: info@homabooks.com
Website: www.homabooks.com

Printed in the U.S.A.
1 3 5 7 9 10 8 6 4 2

Contents

v

Part II

The Author's Preface

The first part of this book is a random compilation of the poems since *Flowers in the Borderland*, that is, the poems published in Korea during the last four years beginning toward the end of 1975 until the middle of 1980; the second, the selected poems from *Well-tempered Clavier* (1968), *Well-Tempered Clavier · 2"* (1972), coauthored with Donggyu Whang, Youngtae Kim, plus some unpublished in any of my previous poetry books.

This book also contains the poems that were translated into English, and published in a poetry magazine of America.

I am deeply grateful to the Moonji Publishers for publishing this poetry book in good speed on behalf of me, who has resided abroad well over a decade now, and humbly dedicate it to my beloved motherland, for her freedom and peace.

Chonggi Mah
The State of Ohio, U.S.A.
June, 1980

PART I

DRAWING

I've taken up drawing.
Decided to be simple like winter.
The tree outside the window's fallen asleep
and images of snow
pile up inside a wanderer's bones.

I've started drawing an urn.
Decided to live like an empty field.
Let the remaining things all rot
into wine for the thirsty
and for sake of love's undergrown grass
began licking
the inward road dark and long.

SECRET OF MANHOOD

Whisper in my ear *It's the end.*
The unfaithful tree forsaken in a field,
it knows, it knows,
the noises from early evening grappling together
crashing, getting hurt, crying.

Everything, if for dear life,
should be terrible, and beautiful.
I too want to caress the soft skin
of love I've risked my life for.

I unfold the wings of manhood
ever flying, to no end,
and shut the window. Shut
all the sorrows of light.

REASON FOR FLOWER · 2

My birth year is 1939 but
where I lived 7 or 8 years before that
misty rain fell for days
you couldn't hear no matter how hard you listened.

I then must have been a window.
I could see a profusion of purple flowers, like mists,
as they were falling in the rain.
I suddenly wished to be a robust man.

DANCE · 5

I've heard a sound
reaching the ear deep and strong
each time the body moved.

I've seen despair of a dancer
who knew of his own pains
but to whom peace was not restored.

I've seen dreams of a dancer,
which diminished the more he writhed,
daubed with thick dark.

Two arms lifted high
two hands spread out
head raised
whole body shaking
It's dark, dark,
shaking, tumbling down
then rising up again.

I've seen liberty of a dancer
shudderingly beautiful,
whole world of stage shaken.
Seen liberty's most fervent face,
color of fire darting from twin eyes.

WIND'S WORD

If, after we have all left,
my soul brush by you
don't ever believe it's the wind
swaying spring twigs.

Today I will plant a flower tree
in a corner of shadowed earth
where I knew you;
when it grows to flower
all our pains acquired from knowing each other
will become petals to fly away.

Become petals to fly away.
Though unbearably faraway and pointless,
are we to live measuring with a ready measure
perhaps all things in the world.
Sometimes inclining your ear windward,
sweet darling, don't forget even when you get tired.
Wind's word coming from far, far away.

WINTER PROMISES

I'll give you a nip
near your middle.
When I reach the age of repose.

I'll stroke down your back
with my sleepless wintry hand
chapped rough even in gloves.
Will stroke long.

Like a heavy snowfall we've breasted each year
I'll overspread you
into the winter night's silence.

My mouth on your ear
your mouth on my neck
I'll show you my song's downy hair, too.

No matter how frigid that winter
I'll let tears mix with tears
and water tremble with water.

BUTTERFLY'S DREAM

1

Let me fly.
It's good and well that I've lived this long.
I'll grow old wandering, crashing.

(A foreign country shines in a brief travel,
good for two-three years' study,
but over ten years, I say, a foreign country gets
really ridiculous and stark.)

A butterfly in dreams, often seen,
a butterfly crossing over the sea
on the wings of time we've wasted,
every day I flew ceaselessly.
A face living undespairing
a music you hear undespairing.

2

Thus undespairing
I want to meet you
at a port in Korea
one rainy evening.
Even though the magnolia standing on a strange road
loses buds in the rain before flowering

and I turn a butterfly in the rain
still I want to meet the day.

A FEW VANITIES

Living in a foreign country well over a decade,
seeing only winds with no fragrance, no direction,
one may get a few cheap vanities.

I want to have rice wrapped in pumpkin leaf.
Till those tiny hairs on steamed pumpkin leaf
get my throat dry.
Live octopus from the open sea of Mokpo, too
lively cuttlefish from the East Sea, too.

When filled, I want to run a marathon as well.
Together with Saechon of the well-house and Kwangsu
    of the fish store
who used to run bare-footed every evening, though it
    was before the 6 · 25,
past Changyung Zoo, Donwha Gate, Chongro 3-ga, 4-
    ga, 5-ga,
then back nearly to the traffic circle in Hyewha-dong,
    all of us out of breath.

If the time now isn't like before
I even want to take a walk.
The back alley of Myeongnyun-dong thick with
    unusually pretty girls,
that alley bustling morning or evening alike.
I want to eat that thick beanpaste soup also.

Now I feel I can understand.
My late father's poverty regretted yet savored
after he threw away everything and returned home,
those few vanities frugally enjoyed.

FROG

1

During my pre-med course I caught a frog and nailed
  him on woodblock, vivisected the belly, fumbled
  with intestines, memorized, *This is kidney, this lung,*
  but really, my finding its internal structure, what
  does it have to do with the frog himself? The frog,
  I suppose, wished over and over to die early.

I went to Bulgwang-dong then a farm, caught and
  boiled a frog, picked bones to bleach, connected
  joints with white nail polish, but I grasp that white,
  beautiful, redolent skeleton also had nothing to do
  with the frog.

Farewell. A few flowers I glimpse, a few flowers that
  bled and withdrew in those times. Oh the beauty
  and courage of us unrefined even after learning we
  had nothing to do with each other. So long!

2

I live like a frog.
Eat when hungry and sleep when night falls,
over the weekend just take
a hot steam bath.

INVISIBLE LAND OF LOVE

Underwater fitly low
hillside fitly high
just count white hair,
just put lotion between fine lines,
practice adapting to circumstances, no need to ponder.

Clearing hoarse voice, cleaning ears,
at times scorching hairy barley
into roasted barley water,
practice living, no telling if I exist or not, just like
    insipid water.

The riddle how I turn a frog
the riddle how a frog grows old.

FIRE IN THE ICE AGE

1

It was overcast every day.
The hand that trimmed stones is frozen,
we see instead stones' sharp tooth
beginning to glint.
The ice age ever so long.
In the lodgings, inescapably
expands the face of ice mountain;
we gather up remnant shadows after burning
and shield our bones
that are noiselessly freezing.

2

Spare, spare,
fire of the age.
There comes a time savage and grim.
Until sharp stone tools become ashes
and conversation between fire and me comes to an end,
our dreams in dark and long nights
not to be cloaked even with primitives' tears.

Don't forget,
a fire burning low comes to the mountaintop,

a fire burning an icy place
is our unending answer.

A JEW'S WINDWOOD INSTRUMENT

At all events I'm against
men killing one another.

Across from me is a man playing oboe
in the spotlight right now
but I'm in hiding among the crowd.

The woodwind notes playing hidden
are sweeter than love
but our classics
first let the hair down and whet the knife.

Winter night, waking up often.
Friend moaning in sleep.

IN SEARCH OF NEW SOUNDS

1. Origin of Sound

Medically speaking, sound
is what blooms
when small and big vibrations of air
move past a bridge of three white bones
and then finally reach clear water.

Precisely speaking, sound
is when your heart's innumerable flutters
return from a long private trip
and then finally opens naked body's vivid eyes.

2. Bird Sound

Listening to the last few autumn leaves that turned little
birds shot and hurling down, reeling bloody, I was
spending dark days in a cave with no one to offer a
hand to lift me up. This year too, I'll be listening
yet again to hard cries freezing on the snow.

3. Water Sound

The boy threw pebbles in the stream all day long. Then
was watching the sound slowly ascending to the
sky. Thoughtfully watching until he could hear in

the evening long shadows of trees caressing, veiling
a tip of the stream, so the sound now sinking not
into the sky but rather into the water.

4. Ecology of Sound

Ever since the sound made when driving a spike into
    palms,
the sound made when driving a spike into folded
    insteps,
the sound of the one who bled
in the mouth lofty and parched, assailed by vertigo

a sound killing another,
a loud sound striking a small one
many small sounds

biting at a loud one,
a falling sound,
a sound shaking another awake
a sound of one quick rising.

Ever since the sound of the bleeding man
the one afflicted merely feels,
affliction makes no sound.

CONCERT · 2
—Perahia the Pianist

Sweetness of sorrows,
sweetness of anticipation,
sweetness of sound
filling up ears,
sweetness of sexual arousal.

Temple and lake and cooking, or
steam in the bathhouse in Myeongnyun-dong some ten
    years ago,
sounds of temple bell and a sylvan view, or
moss on a ginko tree in a suburb of Seoul,
sweetness of a view,
sweetness of auditory hallucination,
sweetness of aroused sound
heard on end deep into the night.

CONCERT · 3

Lately, Maurizio Pollini, or
the surrounding friends' voices
don't just please the ear
but rest on the ends of my hair, like dew.
They cool my brows when I feel gray.

Oh clouds of the many nerves.
What though there once was someone insufferable,
two heedless eyes still moist
wavering but across the waters deep and faraway.

Lately, Maurizio Pollini, or
the surrounding friends' rhythms
testify of me
but with wounds all over the body.

POEM FOR WEDNESDAY

Till poetry becomes a friend
intimate enough at last
to shine a quiet light
so you're not cold in the wind
and not lonely in the night.

Flowers couldn't wait so they bloom
but Wednesdays, each early spring,
I'll be a trustworthy friend and visit,
then I think I'll put ashes on my brows
and laugh away the talk of dying and living.

This thirst from day to day, ever so long,
till the burning fever and meanderings
turn to ashes at last to blow off.

WHEN THE MUSIC I ENJOYED LISTENING TO

When the music I enjoyed listening to becomes a tree
and nods its thousands of bright young leaves,
then, like a bird leaving aloft the oldfangled Western
    skies,
please leave to a forest where more trees crowd and
    clamor
before I settle down peaceful in the shade.

When the music I enjoyed listening to becomes a
    lightning
and lights up by the window on a cold night,
then I see humanity's fire on that awkward night,
our building heated up at our furtive fingertips
and snow to snow, feathery clouds to feathery clouds,
fire making noises, bodies kneading head-to-toe.

A MIDDLE-CLASS FAMILY

Father, since his death, loiters mostly centering around
the Gumgok Cemetery hillside, probably sleepless
worrying about his children sometimes, and
mother, living alone ten-odd years nowadays walks,
I'm told, along the now-someone else's alleyway
where she lived as a newlywed. My younger
brother, an immigrant, haunts the vicinity of Lake
Erie then ludicrously perches himself, they say, and
I wonder what my younger sister's doing in murky
smoke in southern Chicago.

Once we too were a warm middle-class family. We put
our heads together and had salted mackerel pike
for supper, sat around to watch TV drama, once in
a while shared the after-the-meal cookies. A space
of barely over ten years—the decade's bomb put us
asunder and I, a shell splinter, roll about on the
other side of the Pacific Ocean.

That's right. I cannot deny what it means to be a shell
splinter. In a moment of strain vanishes the
glorious hour, and then the abysmal life in which
one's free for he can no longer make a sound, nor
be blown up, nor set afire, so free he cannot be
beautiful. For all that I still cannot deny what is

meant by a shell splinter covered in dust in an unknown land even at high noon.

THE SITE OF GYUNGHAKWON

The site of Gyunghakwon. They tied the innocent
village headman to a withered pine tree, shot him
dead. I saw blood gushing out of his forehead, eyes
open. A sixth grader at an elementary school, I first
watched a man killing another. Although it was
during the 1950-1953 Korean War.

The night before the Recovery of Seoul September 28,
from all around fires flaring up like a great
mountain, I went to the site of Gyunghakwon to
steal bagged rice hidden. Amid the pandemonium
of people fleeing, tumbling down and dying,
shooting, I put rice in a gunnysack and fled. For
we were frightfully famished.

The site of Gyunghakwon, when we returned from a
few years' refuge. Thin pine trees were as before
and it was a bit cold, a bit frightening, but walking
solitary the snowy night I chose to love. Believed
loving everything in the world was the only way to
become a good poet.

The site of Gyunghakwon I visited now and then even
after I became a shoddy poet, an inept doctor.
Bleak and stripped and dust-covered, yet it soothed
me in the glow of my childhood sweat drops; now

when in my vagabond life in a far country to make it worse, I dream of it, then farther and farther comes the precious fond sound calling me *Come, Come,* and in midnight as I awake from a dream, my pillow wet, the site of Gyunghakwon I fasten my eyes on.

AFTER BLESSED DEATH · 4

Every now and then I meet you.
In a strange city in a faraway country
I now live but
among patients who came to me,
similar features, glasses and bald head,
you'd smile but
so glad without a word I cry inside.

From time to time I meet you.
No other way but converse in a foreign language
and though sometimes your skin grows whiter
eyes blue
I know how you, in between patients' pains and fears,
proudly watch me.

You know the pain of watching pain endlessly.
Continuation of fear keeping fear,
when I look lost therein
you come here at your leisure.
Your familiar voice I hear even in the dead of night,
calling me in the rain out the window.

FISHING

Noonday so drowsy even to watch the bob
while fishing,
a thought flashing: why does the fish in that water
live every day?

Why does the fish live?
Why does the earthworm live?
Why does the fish live
just swimming an entire life?

High noon, the whole body suddenly boiling hot
while fishing,
I lay down on the dirt ground of my middle age
and cried like a fish
that no longer can I live just like this.

EVERYDAY FOREIGN COUNTRY

Spring

In the garden untended all winter long
grow tulip stalks.
A woman long-forgotten in my thought
as scent of green grass comes to me.

Summer

Before taking a nap
supine on a flat bench in an islet of the South Sea
I miss
a fly's sound.
Supine on a high-class foreign bed
sleepless,
summer age.

Autumn

By this time, wherever I live,
I hear a cricket sound.
Though a still small voice
the word coming a long way from afar.

Drenched is the hind part
of loneliness I've cloaked

but outside the fence, when it rains,
bloom hibiscuses, too.
You, I still
can hold.

Winter

Evening, snow fallen deep,
a concert in another city.
The pipe organ
even shook anemic entrails.
In the backdrop buried in the snow
was falling low-key notes.

FISH STEW OF PRAGUE

The hope that swept over the city of Prague, Eastern
    Europe,
was soon lost
and Prime Minister Dubcek's smile for freedom
soaked in rainwater, got torn apart.

Springtime, the national flag drops in dark
and a wooden restaurant standing etched.
Blood-spattered flag covered in dust,
I down the fish stew à la Prague
fixed by a short, old Czechoslovakian woman.

Spring rain on the eastern outskirt of Manhattan, New
    York,
starts peering into me again.
(I came to America for grievances but
it's no courage to grow old like this,
the courage to have become a fool is no courage.)

In the eyes of the Czechoslovakian woman, her voice
    croaking,
dissolve the lost son's bones.
The fish stew, needless tongues cut off, and seasoned,
all bones dissolved.
(Must again hold up the flag, again.)

INVISIBLE LAND OF LOVE

1. Hemp Cloth of Okjeo

In a national history class in junior high school I learned of a small country called Okjeo in the land of Hamgyong Province near the east coast. In my dream that night, amid the people of ancient Okjeo was me on a pony, rambling a mountain path. They told me that we were heading for Koguryo, walking idly, some rolled hemp cloth on our ponies. I fretted begrudging that I had suddenly turned a hemp cloth merchant, and, resigned that it's now too late, was crossing over the pass, where wild lettuces were profusely blossoming. At last we reached a large village of another country, and there, a garish golden castle gate opened. And I learned I was to live here away from home thenceforth, I though can't remember why. Afraid that I'd have to live by myself in this vast place even though my father and mother didn't seem like natives of Okjeo, I buried my face in the hemp cloth bundle and gulped down my tears. That fish-like odor from the bundle I still cannot forget. As though relieved by the odor, I kept taking my leave of whomever, Goodbye, goodbye. Making wrong steps for I couldn't see anything. Before I knew it I was one from Okjeo, clad in hemp clothing. Long ago in a national history class I learned of a small country called Okjeo.

2. River in Kihae Year 1839*
—Sorrows flow out of flesh and blood.
Changheum Choi, the blessed martyr of 1839*

This province's winds grow under the dark river,
this province's flesh and blood is where winds pull.
Outside Seosomun, the blood splashing in Senamteo
    forms a river,
desiccated souls wake up in the river water of former
    age.
Invisible people who believe an invisible land.

Huigwangi, twain-eyes-wide-open Hwigwangi,
19th century Korea's mad executioner,
Close your eyes, A neck drops, Eyes drop.
A river with longevity is a river without scent.
Sounds of rain falling on the severed head
are a land's perpetual sorrows.

*The year 1839, in Korean almanac, is Kihae Year.
*Changheum Choi, baptismal name Peter, was
    martyred in 1839 and later canonized.

3. Dialogue

Dad, aren't you afraid?
No. It's dark.
Where are you going now?
I'll have to go and see.
This doesn't mean we won't see each other at all?
No. We'll meet now and then.
Only in the dark like this?
No. Will see in the light also.
Are you going to your country?
To me, it's friendly there anyway.
You've had no fun here?
I have, too.
Then why go?
I'm afraid I'll be lonelier anyway.
Can you be lonely when you die?
All the same. Dark.
You like a country where you don't have your own
    house or car?
You see, it's my native land.
So many countries out there, what's the big deal?
'Cause Grandfather's there.
Didn't he pass away?
He's still there.
Is that all?
I've got friends, too.
You think some of them still remember you?
Let's say, No, but I still have friends.

What's the point of having friends who don't even
    remember you?
'Cause I love'em.
Love can grow anywhere, don't you think?
It doesn't seem to live just anywhere.
So, have you written poems to remember love?
To make a light, it was dark.
Is a poem a light?
To me, it was a lamplight.
But you were still dark, weren't you?
The lamp went out again and again.
Can you see the land you love?
I've got my lamp.
But it's so far away that you can't see, can you?
I've got my lamp.

−Dad, go, and make sure to be back. What you've
    looked for may not be. But do look for it. And
    then, Dad, wander no more, please.

−The snow falling all night long has finally stopped. I
    am on my way once more. Heaven and earth piled
    high with snow ever since I left my homeland, it's
    hard to tell a single footmark of mine but I arise
    and start out, before I turn insipid water to sink to
    the ground.

PART **II**

WINTER'S TALE

How has winter come?
In the bleak garden falls early dark
and sounds of the river that glimmered cease,
white frost on the cheek.

It was bound for Oijeongbu,
when it snowed unexpectedly
the Revelation of John joggling
in the last night bus,
the Grave of Lady Seo of Eechon, the faithful daughter-
    in-law
all night in the snow.

So too, silent tears streaking down
at end of a smile of an old man dying a blessed death.
Like the speed of those tears, as yet
the winter's tarrying solitary.

STATISTICS

My statistics in 1966:
murders of some 50 people
death certificates of some 200.
Wait to see how they draw their last breaths,
people are all the same.
I've seen they look genuinely lonely.
Shedding a line of tears, they part.

My foreign country in 1966:
the hand of self-awareness frozen in deep snow
I walk this street of actual proof,
the sign of cigma now hidden in my body.

LOVE SONG · 9

1

I live
bidding farewell.

A dead friend quietly comes
to whisper in my ear
under water on a spring day,
Dying and living is like water sound.

Is that so, the spring day already darkening,
I learn privily
the endings of those friends' lonesome smile.

2

May, during my medical school course, toward dark
    daybreak after a vigil in the anatomy classroom
    lined with corpses, I confessed my innocent love.
    Amid whispers of dim lightbulbs and corpses, us in
    our gowns smeared with human flesh.

Before that year was over the corpses dissolved, love
    vanished, and I, waxing older but not growing,
    walked on, getting acquainted with indoor
    wanderings, indoor quiet. The youngish patient

who would like some black tea became a melted-
up sound the next day; I standing afar had
something to think about.

3

When there's a friend
I asked,

About the meaning of evening after one whole day's
    torture,
the sight of one's back walking offhandedly.

About the blank list I had
in the night when I happened to wake,
about the sound of forlorn night calling.

Our innards
sank deep under water and
I asked
about that smile I was anticipating.

LOVE SONG · 10

1

Living in a lodging house in this substandard city, let me go ahead and watch a Walt Disney's animated film in the evening. The room is so lax I was robbed of everything, this heated movie theatre befits my state. I also turn a grasshopper in a world of all colors, the snow falls nonstop outside, and alone I watch, alone I come home, my feet chilled.

2

Walking about the library I unthinkingly pick a respiratory, internal medicine book; on the cover is a signature of R. K. Alexandria and written with a pen—Boston, Massachusetts, August 2, 1879. August 2, 1879 was overcast. Faded letters written with a pen, I stare at the hand marks of the internist Mr. Alexandria gone to grave. In my book I write down 1966, I too will be a great internist.

3

When I own a porched house I was going to fix a soft-sounding doorbell and welcome a friend dropping by. Going to love winter, writing a letter in a blue aerogramme; wear rimless glasses and let my beard grow just a bit, and then read in a placidly calm voice *Augustus* by Hesse. Now you've come to find out. What's left is a conversation for six months at the longest; you've found out my six months' love, six months' world, six months' evenings, and six months' heartbreaking left for me, six months' tears.

DANCE
—To Mrs. Pouline Koner

I too have fallen in love
akin to your dance.
A single movement
stayed deep in my breast
so for the weight I bowed my head,
was it spring, or autumn,
I too wearing that absurd expression
of the artist you respect
have mounted stairs
to make a visit.
Your motionless dance,
silent music,
I've fallen in love without regard
as your dance which is nonetheless replete.

DANCE · 2

1

You dance
bare-footed all along
but my mother,
shod in shoes from Relief Mission, purchased
in the West Gate market,
winter snow falling in sheets,
stepped on in the commuter bus,
mother lost in the dance, as in a dream.

2

Involuntary muscles contract.
While in college ill with stomach ulcer
our interlude was long
and all our plans rooted out.
Tens of thousands megavolt of static heat
converging in your lifted two arms.

3

Be sure to establish the time and place of encounter
before raising the stage curtain.
Getting out of illuminated urban streets,
out of life's radius

so narrow as it was,
angels' amusement.

DISCHARGE FROM HOSPITAL

In midsummer about a decade before
I left the hospital.
In midsummer about a decade before
when bright sunlight smiled at me
and even the city's din was like a happy melody
I learned gratitude.

Summer flowers smile.
Now a doctor myself
in a ward in a foreign country
I give flowers to the patient who's leaving the hospital.
Invisible flowers,
I pass on my smile
of the midsummer about a decade before.

So my flower took a long journey.
Thou bestow meaning upon all those flowers.
Blowing, falling, fructifying,
thy fragrance.

POET'S ROOM

Light up the 19th century candle then take off the lustrous, unfinished wooden desk, then the poet's room is a brood hen's gizzard; it's a brood hen that has Monsieur Chagall's pearl. Small, vermilion eyes.

So the venerable monsieur worked as a postmaster in France for some years, and now defunct, was raising chickens back at home. The poet's room is the postcard of Frankfurt am Main; the poet's room an odd stamp of Europe.

When I collapse from exhaustion in a special military training, still wearing my trench helmet marked with red cross, and the night dew wakes me out of a light sleep, then the poet's room is a greenhouse for tropical plants; my lover on a trip to the Mediterranean Sea mailed me a package of two pebbles ripened up in the sun.

Never was there a time when we paid no respect to a hermit's eye, but, one dark summer daybreak as I opened my eyes alone in a mountain path, I couldn't help thinking of a hermit's dulled senses—a love withering even in memory.

True. We have an addiction that once brightened world. Monsieur Chagall's postcards or two pebbles. I can but contemplate the use of my poet still warm notwithstanding.

WINTER'S TALE · 3

Missing the flat stone floor that smells scorched
under a padded comforter in the room opposite the
    living room,
missing the brow-chilling draft
that sweep over the two rooms,
wishing for deviation,
missing the miniscule face of *maehwa**
feeding on wintry dust near the foot of our bed,
missing the old twain cranes on the wardrobe
on the wing after oversleeping,
I go out,
then missing the mold inside the *kimchi** jar,
yes, toxic mold from Joseon Dynasty
on crouching knees.
Father before winter came;
the little finger
of a nobleman, shaking
over the straight-down dominoes.

*maehwa is a Japanese apricot.
*kimchi is a staple vegetable dish in Korean diet, the
    equivalent of western salad.

ILLUSTRATION · 1
-Born in Louisville, Kentucky, 29 years old
-Single white man
-Confirmation of death: November 3, 1966

When you lived
talked and smiled
I in my large gown
thought of *Kimchi*.
When you lived
bragged your blond photo
I thought of my mother.
When you died
six feet out the window the dawn took leave on foot
and I with one minute's examination
confirm the death.
Life is to live unawares
then to give it back.
The hospital yard where all night rain stopped,
a lustrous tree,
I turn all of a sudden and see you.

ILLUSTRATION · 2

Summer evening, old lady Braishire, my neighbor, perched on a wicker chair, told me the history of immigration to America. Educated in New York City, her cheerless articulation conveying even some geniality behind glasses, her successful child now away from her, in the second-floor room where she lives by herself are photos of glory days.

So it was when her critical condition was notified. Colorful cards and an air-mailed bouquet bright in the setting sun, but no visitor for the old lady— you, a patient of mine who's an alien physician. My eyes perceive the solitude of a great country. Even when I on the cold steel dissecting table cut the brain, excoriate the face and eviscerate, my eyes perceive your solitude with lips shut mute.

I know all my patients most deeply. I hear dark confessions in the sick room, hear the last burning desire and death approaching. And then when death has come slowly, or suddenly, I cut apart the body to detect the cause of the disease, finally insert my long silence into the utterly desolate space of abdominal cavity and close the door.

Oh human being, beloved sweet human being. No
longer can I remember you by the blood which
enlivened limbs of the dead. When someday there
blooms in our abdominal cavities nameless
mountain flowers and transformed lives grow anew,
then this world's unruly winds ruled over, we will
meet again. Meet in a rivulet in a valley, oh human
being.

ILLUSTRATION · 5

1

It was not just because of my misdiagnosis that you died, but when you went home to the funeral parlor from Ward #12 I had neither strength nor courage to go home. Please forgive.

The real misdiagnosis was that I became a doctor. So many miscalculations in the high school arithmetic exams were a test case, so to speak, but your death only sets a cold tombstone.

Should you ever see in an alleyway of your lifetime, or in a dream, one who says he lives remorseful, please forgive. Your remorse is shared in my breast. Even so, night comes faster than penance.

2

When I pass by the public cemetery
it always smells of mint.
A square window redolent of mint,
the dawn outside that window
needs to practice to see the inside.
No ceiling, no floor, no corner,
the phenomenon of ionization of an individual.

In the night I shall again set my eyes
on that vivid body raised;
I'll sometime wash my hands deep
to find your fingerprint therein.

ILLUSTRATION · 6
—To Baby Ann Saunders

Before I became a daddy to a baby, a patient, whether old or young, was just a patient; before I became a daddy I, like a machine, treated him and the crying irritated me imperceptibly; before I became a daddy to a baby growing day to day, never once burgeoned in my worthless doctor's eyes a small blossom of pity.

After sticking in the breast bone a spikelike needle to finally diagnose a disease which wouldn't let you live long, I stayed out of your sick room, and when you beckoned, cheeks feverish, I once again became a stranger in a daze. Then one day, when you died in my irrelative arms, I finally saw you sweetly alive. Ah, now painfully budding. My pains, translated into water sounds, murmur day and night.

Don't hate, baby. Don't hate the research by spirited philosophers who hold that when one dies at a place on earth all ends for him. You are better than they. The older one grows, so much the more forgetfulness, and eyes that see but the visible grow dim. They scorn, but baby, you on your death proved again to me. Alive or dead, we do not part.

TOY

My childhood toys
at the close of the Second World War
became trash
and during the 6 · 25
I ate pumpkin porridge
and played kneading mud.
The clouds in summer sky
as I gazed up, famished.

My baby,
baby welcoming daddy
coming home from work, slump-shouldered,
the smile in your eyes now
is my only toy
and I am an empty bed of grass
where I roll your toy.

An empty bed of grass
that cannot easily fall asleep
even after you did.

CONCERT

1

On the back of Debussy
falls snow again.
Bosom friends from the 1950s
shuffling off closet loneliness
detect a lily.
Young women at large,
Oriental or European,
are more glamorous naked
but I settle
on a blond flower younger than a lily.

2

David Oistrakh, now a young man,
steals out of the concert,
with a violin-shaped tennis racket
vigorously plays tennis.
I challenge decisively.
During the break
I mop my palms
soaked in wartime sweat.

3

When I was in the army, drinking heavily,
powdered orphans
came to comfort me, singing in unison.
A neck-straining steel helmet on,
I was unjustly comforted.
Watched Gustav Mahler's ghost
already turned into coal
and burning bright in flames
in the red-hot stove in the night duty room,
stealthily awaited that the blaze would spread
also on the earth frozen hard and fast.

IN THE BATHHOUSE

Water washes water.
Soft water
rubs against firm water.
Rubs against
your soft body.

Our love too
was water.
Curves of the flesh
visible in winter,
loneliness not quite visible.

Like the rainbow
that escapes the Myeongnyun-dong alley
on Sunday afternoon as the rain dries up
after the bath,
like the rainbow of about five colors,
like giddiness light and bright.

Water washes water.
Transparent water
rubs against
nontransparent water.

Time's past and present
murmuring, sounds of bathwater;

every part of my flesh
becoming again cold and transparent water
then falling on Myeongnyun-dong 2-ro, or 3-ro,
the midwinter snow.

Our love too
was water.
The warmth still remaining
in the body weight now.

DUAL EVERYDAY LIVES

After an unusual evening
I drink in Bach's music
afloat in a cup of coffee.

A great distance
one notices
only after several years in the West.

Such a distance from here,
a paddy field at one end of Jeolla-do,
whose surface parched in drought
comes to life out of old newspaper
to suddenly become my brother.

Dead or alive, brother,
your shadow's long and lean
That changeless shadow
hastily shoved in a pocket
I attend a party where the ceiling's high.

At night
I take out my rumpled shadow
and try waving it
like a forgotten banner.

Lately I experience to the point of discomfort
a pocket rather great in size,
the music of my own shadow.

TO MR. JAMES MILLER

Don't tell me you know Yeungdeungpo.
It isn't the Yeungdeungpo
that ends up with your subtle smile.
There may be Youngja Sunja Bongsun there
but it isn't the Yeungdeungpo
that ends up with dear mama and so-and-so.

Take refuge, hang about in the marketplace,
fill your stomach with pigswill, then you'll know.
Tomato and lumps of meat and paper scraps altogether,
the slop churning and heaving your bowels,
you know since you've savored the taste.

The return to Seoul, aboard a dilapidated train,
pledging, Never more suffering,
though it was dark and the train stalled long
but the permit, permit, river-crossing permit,
the pale hope for me, ten-something,
abides still there on and on.

Don't tell me you know Yeungdeungpo.
There must have sprung up a cheery wig factory
and they say an overhead crossing is good for driving
but in the Yeungdeungpo for three years of my military
     life
there was but *makkolli** and chill.

INVISIBLE LAND OF LOVE

Rampant was anxiety and inferiority complex, drooping
     in rain water,
and nightly I chucked up my groundless mental
     disorder,
arrogantly booted all meaning,
then, ashamed, blanketed myself in the closet;
our youth which was truly rare and dense.
Our chilliness, now lost,
must be still hanging about
near tumbledown sidewalk and stationery.

Don't tell me you know Yeungdeungpo.
Several years already since I left my homeland,
all of Mr. Millers,
my excited quivering voice
loses balance before your twenty-year old hot blood.

Makkolli is crude rice wine.

POEMS OF CHONGGI MAH

AFTER BLESSED DEATH · 1

1

Gourd flower, I see, covertly blows by night only.
Grown older, the full moon growing bright,
father's insomnia late in life
is pretty palpable in his rice water bowl,
sending me into gloom
covertly out of sight.

In winter, I see, he shuts double paper door,
his fingertips again and again
picking out powdery ashes in the earthen brazier.
Put out the light, let's sleep now.
An annihilation of the smoke of ambitions great and
small
in a world so dark it's obscure.

2

I see you.
I see you.
Murmurs of low-hanging mists
on a spring morning in an alien land far away,
a bird
brushing up with two hands

67

boundless solitude that diffused overnight
then soaring up Sunday morning.

AFTER BLESSED DEATH · 2

1

A wild flower beckoning small
around the sod where you're laid down tired,
then at nighttime your soul for a while
strolls over to an edge of my desk
to confer me a word.
Breathing smooth, over a long way,
you smile
so much clearer, lighter than this world's sounds.
Your graceful golden age
beheld so much nearer to the end of my life.

2

I turn my back.
Turn my body
away from the import of all things.
Cool bed
finishes off a dream I grudge missing.
Be cool-headed.
Be cool-headed to your dream.
A sudden uncharted land
splendidly rises upon my breast.

AFTER BLESSED DEATH · 3

Your smile
is an inorganic matter.
It won't burn in fire,
even when buried underground
becomes an immortal piece of music
unalterable by any means,
to be played in great depth.

Your smile
is outside the window of my living room.
When I see you from within
you become grass, become tree,
become wind, mist and sky, too;
your smile
is my landscape
that encompasses far wherever I go.

THE STARE

North of Ward 2 to which I go down, there in a chair
is a blind girl always sitting like a picture
smiling, both hands folded.
A footfall, then a smile of the seventeen-something,
what's the girl seeing every day
in the dark hallway north of Ward 2.
I was looking at a plane.
I was looking at a book.
No, I was looking at legs.
Drinking liquor and taking pants off the other,
no, I was watching water.
From morning cold rain falling on the traffic circle in
    Yeungdeungpo,
and I, under a vinyl umbrella,
breaking out in a cold sweat for hangover from last
    night
was watching rain water
puddling, and muddying my army shoes.
Everything quickly got heavy
and for a long time, really long time, I
was looking down at rain water.

AND THEN A PEACEFUL AGE

And then comes a peaceful age, I see.
Tee-dum-dum, we hear the drumbeat of previous age
and curfew bells resound in heaven and earth
and great brothers clasping shoulders cry, I see.
Our forefathers who used the selfsame language
    thousands of years
I see, shake off dust to rise up.
In the sea, in the land, from all quarters
I see, blind and deaf and dead ghosts
out of their mind again give cheers.
The land overflows, I see, with great anticipation
and unaccustomed heaps of flowers piling,
the peninsula's middle, giddy, takes a tumble.

I was born, raised abroad,
spent adolescence in my motherland,
and now am again out in an alien land.
The memory of the summer of my adolescence
is dead bodies slain by guns and spears:
a thousand, ten thousand, a million bodies
dead and rotten, seething in wells,
stacked like firewood, burned into char
so my adolescence charred
and even 20 years later, at dawn, in dreams,
it plunges down into a well,
at the injurers' low-keyed chorus

gooseflesh all over my adolescent body.
Should you look at the globe just for one night,
measure, and examine again
you'll see how disgraceful your greedy eyes are
in the fair land smaller than a little fingernail.
Look again and ask again.
A country more miserable than us,
count those miserable countries.
You may beat your breast but I'm to be blamed for
    failure.
We're to be blamed for misery.

Awake from early morning hagridden dream
I feel traces of tears unforeseen.
Who could keep away each and all dust of snow?
Corpses in every nook and cranny of the land,
from their bone ashes and eyeballs we'll gather yellow
    phosphor, red phosphor
and kindle millions of candles
that keep dying out, then lighting up—

And then, I see, comes a peaceful age.
The land of Goguryeo as well as the plains of Balhae
given away for you're good-hearted,
the Neutral Zone now turned into a National Natural
    Park,
I see rabbits running the park.

ALLEGORICAL RIVER

One person meets another, each growing fond of the
    other,
then opens between the two a waterway.
One side is saddened, then the friend's heart aches;
with waves of joy the waterway so sparkles
his laughter is heard all the way to the river mouth.

The early waterway being brief and awkward
each must send own water, often mingle together,
the flow of devotion through life long and winding
    can't be ordinary,
a magnificent river not overflowing nor failing can't be
    ordinary.

No superfluous words, it's already grasped by the flow;
no gathering for years, the river has no trouble sleeping
    at night,
surely how could a great river be in a flow signifying
    nothing.
Meeting another in the world and liking for long,
how could that be simple and light as dying and living.

A great river from start to finish we can't tell any way,
    but
I wish to be acquainted with a person who asserts own
    waterway ever clear.

Thou watching over me when my soul slumbers,
the thought of thee always recalling a river full of life,
I wish to stay close to such a one pleasant and fair.

LECTURE ROOM 3

Preface I

It happened years ago, when I began to feel uneasy and
stayed up all night, eyes open. As my friends,
alumni of four-year university, upon graduation,
were talking composedly about society, I myself
invited insomnia to fill up the time deprived due
to silly wandering and drinking, and thus keeping
up my record. However, I practically didn't yet
know much about the world.

1

One autumn afternoon, the sun beating down hot, I
was in Lecture Room 3 upstairs—attending an
obstetrics lecture at a desk 20-or-30 years old, my
brain honed 20-or-30 years.
Just in time, the baby, head bent in mother's pelvis,
outwardly came full circle, and then was thrusting
out its head; the mother had to suffer in that
peculiar fashion the pain of being stretched out ten
centimeters in diameter. But the birth of one life
being more precious than that pain, at last it bursts
out crying, enveloped in mother's pain in her place.
Mother!

Is it that a human being, then, is thus engendered to overflow ever more on earth, and the sun beats down hot in order to bring me to maturity? If you observe closely once more you'd lose a bit of the world, and the baby experience that pain again?

2

The lecture room of several years ago where I was attending lectures was the locale about a thousand of my seniors went through over five decades, I guess you remember—. Absorbed in the lecture (absorption, I'm told, is healthful), I leaned against the wall. The wall took away restlessness; it was deferring my leap toward the unknown. A fly out of season, startled, fled in between mother and baby, and the wall continued to touch the body and the head cold.

Then I came to a sudden realization that the other side of the wall I was leaning against was the Human Anatomy Lab, in which corpses are lying abreast. The place where my future friends who taught me drinking and smoking, wrote poems again amid all that, and brought forth religion, were lying— corpses fit to make a young lady a realistic artist when she, a student of art, mixes enough of purple and dirt-black hues and paint withal—though she ends up failing frequently as she doesn't believe

she'd be one herself—behold. The best clothes for
stately lives.

3

The ceiling plaster somehow peeled off so the
sophisticated shape all the more suggested an
engraving; swarms of so many flies, sucking human
flesh, were spewing restlessness saturated in human
flesh. By the way, aha, one, two, and one more—I
notice yellow sunbeams dancing; I think it's those
guys' doing.

The backside of the class room, just out the window
was an alley. The alley as convoluted as our nerves,
amid the army tent-turned-into-roof barrack, I
mean, the shacks. Looking down, several meters
below, it's again these guys. I guess you remember
far better, the ladies, having few clients during the
daytime, don't even wash their faces when they
awake in the morning and are in this same old
game as ever. The fact of the matter was that a
ruined woman, a piece of mirror in hand, was
reflecting sunbeams into the class room. Come
down! Come Down! Free for you! She meant she'd
learn from clients busily in and out through the
night singing the praise of springtime, and then
teach us. Come down! Come down!

Eyeing the sunlight's enchanted play, we began to feel
enlivened, our eyes brightening up in a pleasant

mood as when listening to Mozart's clarinet. Come
down! Come down! Well, come down, I say! We
could not yet hear the music, relaxed farther off,
just as we'd hear others talking.

4

Obstetric session eventually ended, leaving behind a
question: how to shrewdly sleep all curled up,
while watching the ill-gotten pregnant woman
having a difficult childbirth. As the session was
ending, the rain started. When I'm done with
whatever, my habit, though, starts over again.
Of course, that fall I wasn't quite as perky as to go see
the colored autumn leaves. At dreary rain sound
the cheerful Come-down girls were gone into their
dream palace, and over there below the window
was heard a singing that tugged at my heartstrings.
I think it came from the pathology / autopsy room
in the slant, single story building. An oldish
indigenous *Choson* woman and a student appearing
to have just turned twenty were singing, Dear
Soon, dear, both their hands on the red brick wall,
tapping, and keeping time.
In this Lecture Room 3 we, however, have heard such a
song once or twice a day for so many days. Initially
it choked me awhile, and then it made me
solemnly contemplative, then past that, I was as
heedless as to wonder if I had become a deaf, an

idiot; but recently my ears are open at last to pick up the tune. Such music, shall we say, as you hear in the wilderness of Central Asia. But rain fell; autumn was so mellow that each tree-leaf got glass beads; I unexpectedly felt the surge of lyricism from my childhood. Dear Soon, dear Soon, when you and I live together let's spend our time with a smile every day. To me, who stammered when speaking in my mother-tongue, there was but one pretty Soon. Alas, alas, poor, dear Soon—the hoarse voice of the child's mom was old and weak but her crying was pulsing through rain-sodden long locks and white cotton skirt.

The dovelike child died first, and in the autopsy room my senior laid Soon on the autopsy table, sawed her chest to extract lungs and heart, sawed skeletal bones, and now was lifting brain. (When I touched brain, however, I always mistook it for tofu and used to cut feeling good). Puddles of blood recalled a day of Soon's life. Do you know what a sophisticated person the female doctor, who's entering with a chopping board to shred the liver, is? Dating in full swing these days, she's getting a kick out of it. Luckily it was raining hard, weary mother-and-son's crying stopped and the lady doctor, walking autumnal streets in a raincoat, was already feeling in the liver the body heat they're going to share. She is obviously a free patient so it

was a helpless business. No doubt the law was
protecting everyone safe.

5

The lecture ended, and I had to slip out of Lecture
Room 3, with my bag. Today, first of all I had to
give a friend an SM* shot, who's sitting cross-
legged in the closet, and then see my childhood
girlfriend who was leaving for the New World.
This girlfriend was simply cute and lovely
everywhere when I was younger, then years later
dashing ahead of me, finally turned out gorgeous.

Rummaging in my pocket, I said I'd better buy a vinyl
umbrella, but for this girlfriend a vinyl umbrella
would be a wrong thing so I could not but hesitate.
Nonetheless, I always hesitated before this
girlfriend, so it dawned on me this vinyl umbrella
would be just the thing for me instead.

All of a sudden, transmigration! As babies still continue
to be born anew in Lecture Room 3 and "Come
down girls" on a full stomach sing up in pop-song
style the heyday of youth, corpses would pray
toward the ceiling, looking as if somewhat scornful
of the world—and the mother and son still leaning
against the wall of autopsy room; about when
would they end the finale of death and the little
girl, but suddenly transmigration!

I hesitated again then felt a sharp hunger more than transmigration. You see, it was a scientific era then, when they launched satellites. The bag in my hand, I folded the vinyl umbrella hesitant as I was and got in a *Makkolli* bar. As though that was my lecture room there......

*SM here is the abbreviation of streptomycin.

Preface II

Now the friend waiting for me in the closet will get pristine springtime afresh, and the pious prayer will awake to take the little girl who long ago dreamed with me. Yet feeling something missing, she'll linger awhile in that tea house, then leave. Will surely smile and leave in the end.

Indeed, you've waited quite a while. You students, who are in the lecture room broiling cow's small intestine sizzling hot. Right now, the rain's coming down in buckets outside. They'll have to set up a roadblock; I'll stay, drinking the rest of *Makkolli*. When this rain stops I'll grow a little bit more. Of course, I'm dreadfully ignorant of the world yet—. You've waited quite a while indeed.

COMMENTARY

Warm Heart, Warm Poems
—On Reading Recent Poems of Chonggi Mah

Joo Youn Kim

1

Don't forget,
a fire burning low comes to the mountaintop,
a fire catching an icy place
is our unending answer.
—"Fire in the Ice Age"

One day in June, feeling so dejected I didn't feel like holding a pen even, then came poems of Chonggi Mah across the sea and I read. I spent one whole month plus a week— in an unbounded nadir of nihility where one doesn't even want to read someone else's writing! I hope you wouldn't laugh. Early summer of 1980 is intolerably futile. Nearly forty now, I seem to grasp for the first time the reality of nihility which Nietzsche beheld with a scowl, Ben with a cold stony look. This disgrace to barely sense the life of the word *nihility* among the many pains of life! And then the first thing I read is none other than this *Invisible Land of Love* by him. Sweet poem, beautiful poem, sad poem, easy and honest poem no one can reject. This time his poetry specially brings a lump to my throat. Pain quite like a sharp knife cutting into the flesh, or vehement passion whose deep voice stirs up one's whole body, are a far cry from his poetry. So tender and sensitive as to evoke a sentimental sensation is his poetic mood.

> I unfold the wings of manhood
> ever flying not to cease,
> and shut the window. Shut
> all the sorrows of light.

This is the last part of a poem entitled "Secret of Manhood." There's no word difficult to understand, nor a shadow of ideological abstrusity. The word *ideological* has primarily nothing to do with this poet. Some parts too easy, some parts laced with overmuch commonly-used words, they occasion an impression of banality rather. The above quotation from "Secret of Manhood" could be said a close example. But, first, read the previous part of this poem, then one is bound to acknowledge that such feeling was hasty.

> Whisper in my ear It's the end.
> The unfaithful tree forsaken in a field,
> it knows, it knows,

the noises grappling together
crashing, getting hurt, crying.

Everything, if for dear life,
should be terrible, and beautiful.
I too want to caress the soft skin
of love I've risked my life for.

This is a poem with no particular content to speak of. It may be truthful to say this is a poem without a subject, rather than without "content." The expression like "I too want to caress the soft skin / of love I've risked my life for" evokes astonishing emotion. Consider how the intensity / ferocity produced by "love I've risked my life for" is exquisitely reversed, and thus consoled. Such technique as this is no mere skill of elementary wording. It has to accompany a mind that can control it. Chonggi Mah decisively has it. One opens the surface of his words seemingly as plain delicate as of a young lady of literary interest only to see coiling therein pains of life and times one cannot resist; and when the pains are on the verge of sobbing his congenial, overcoming wisdom to quickly stay it. This mind, and his techniques, are this poet's charm. One can say that this is a certain state he has reached through extensive experience of a poet over two decades, but, as for me, I wish to say that is an original triumph of poetry stemming from a warm heart, which can be attributed to Chonggi Mah's inherent nature.

2

Most of Chonggi Mah's poems' subjects are personal. Not only in poetry but in literature as a whole, the term "personal" is not so good. No doubt a literary work is a story of the writer, namely the author, yet it should not be of himself alone, that is, personal. Because something personal simply concerns himself only and therefore inhibits another's empathy. If one should define the story of the writer himself, which is not just of himself, as generality, this distinct generality perhaps is the greatest virtue a writer must possess. While a work ambiguous about the persona lacks concreteness, an autobiographic work will descend to a personal level; thus a writer's competency rests in overcoming this dilemma. The fact that Chonggi Mah's poems are personal lies in that his subjects, however, are certainly personal. In a strict sense, that's not yet personal. Therefore, what I wish to declare is: this poet's world so abounding with his own stories that whoever reads might get an impression of its being personal, is not in the least personal indeed. It's true that the subjects of Mah's poems at first blush certainly give an impression of being personal.

Father, since his death, loiters mostly centering
    around Gumgok Cemetery hillside,
probably sleepless worrying about his children
    sometimes, and mother, living alone
ten-odd years nowadays walks, I'm told, along the
    now-someone else's alleyway
where she lived as a newlywed. My younger
    brother, an immigrant, haunts the
vicinity of Lake Erie then ludicrously perches
    himself, they say, and I wonder what
my younger sister's doing in murky smoke in
    southern Chicago.

This first part of "A Middle-Class Family" barely
retaining poetic structure is a family story of the poet
himself. His "private circumstances" as such are
specifically focused on the facts that the poet's
occupation is medical doctor, and that he has left his
homeland and is now in a foreign country. 'Doctor'
and 'diasporic life' definitely comprise two
momentous motifs to this poet. Pervasive is the motif
of 'doctor.'

During my pre-med course I caught a frog and
    nailed him on woodblock,
vivisected the belly, fumbled with intestines,
    memorized, This is kidney, this lung, but
really, my finding its internal structure, what does
    it have to do with the frog himself.

The frog, I suppose, wished over and over to die
      early. (1)

Medically speaking, sound
is what blooms
when small and big vibrations of air
move past a bridge of three white bones
and then finally reach clear water. (2)

From time to time I meet you.
In a strange city in a faraway country
I now live but
among patients who came to me
similar features, glasses and bald head,
you'd smile but
so glad without a word I cry inside. (3)

My statistics in 1966:
murders of some 50 people
death certificates of some 200.
Wait to see how they draw their last breaths,
people are all the same,
I've seen they look genuinely lonely.
Shedding a line of tears, they part. (4)

May, during my medical school course, toward
      dark daybreak after a vigil in the
anatomy classroom lined with corpses, I've
      confessed my innocent love. Amid whispers

of dim lightbulbs and corpses, us in our gowns
smeared with human flesh. (5)

As I continued to read his works in sequence, I
randomly selected parts of "Frog" (1), "Origin of
Sound—in search of new sounds" (2), "After Blessed
Death · 4" (3), "Statistics" (4), "Love Song · 9" (5).
These works are regarded to have a doctor motif, and
here the common denominator, if any, is that one can
hardly see an ostentatious depiction of the occupation
of doctor, or of being a doctor himself. Though
already a great doctor of good standing, the doctor
motif is linked with the state of shock he was in
roughly at the outset of his medical study. From the
time of a pre-med student, considered an incipient
stage for a doctor, he already complains the
meaninglessness, futility, of frog dissection, and
frustration with life (1) "Frog". In (2) his medical
knowledge is utilized with a trace of pride, a rare
thing in this poet, which is employed as a means to
attempt to distill the essence of sounds—the poet sees
life therein. On the other hand, (3) is a depiction of a
doctor, an everyday man in his casual time, who
misses his late father. The works in which one
glimpses a concise determination not to despair or go
insane, and instead to hold on to a warm cord of life,
even though he feels keenly the vacuity of life, are
"Statistics" (4), "Love Song · 9" (5), and so forth.
What one feels while reading these works containing

hardly any difficulty is the fact that the doctor motif goes far beyond personal interests. We come to realize that therein lies hidden a warm heart that through a healing process overcomes those materialistic concerns, which makes the body a sole subject, or those utilitarian concerns, thus replacing pain with love. Such overcoming disposition likewise is found in 'life in a foreign country,' regarded as another personal motif.

> Living in a foreign country well over a decade,
> seeing only winds with no fragrance, no direction,
> one may get a few cheap vanities.

> I want to have rice wrapped in pumpkin leaf.
> Till those tiny hairs on steamed pumpkin leaf
> get my throat dry.
> Live octopus from the open sea of Mokpo, too
> lively cuttlefish from the East Sea, too. (1)

> That's right. I cannot deny what it means to be
>   shell splinter. In a moment of strain
> vanishes the glorious hour, and then the abysmal
>   life for one's free as he can no longer
> make a sound, nor be blown up or set afire, so free
>   he cannot be beautiful. Yet I
> cannot deny what is meant by shell splinter
>   covered in dust in an unknown land even
> at high noon. (2)

Before taking a nap
supine in a flat bench in an islet of the South Sea
I miss
a fly's sound.
Supine in a high-class foreign bed
sleepless,
summer age. (3)

Summer flowers smile.
Now a doctor myself
in a ward in a foreign country
I give flowers to the patient who's leaving the
    hospital.
Invisible flowers,
I pass on my smile
of the midsummer about a decade before. (4)

I selected these works also as I read on by their
sequence; they are parts of "A Few Vanities" (1), "A
Middle-Class Family" (2), "Everyday Foreign
Country" (3), "Leaving the Hospital" (4). (1) literally
talks of a longing for motherland, a factual byproduct
of diasporic life, and we note this life is defined
"winds with no fragrance, no direction." That life
may not have such a thing as direction, but does it
not have at least some "fragrance"? The poet, however,
seems not to think so. The last part provides a good
evidence.

Now I feel I can understand.
My late father's poverty regretted yet savored
after he threw away everything and returned home,
those few vanities frugally enjoyed.

What can exactly be a few vanities? Couldn't they actually be some fragrance one encounters in diasporic life? But, according to him, they are merely "cheap vanities." Vanities his late father "frugally enjoyed in poverty" is the reality of the home faced after renouncing diasporic life then returning thither, that is, his own reality mirrored once more. It is an image of an affectionate individual who lives holding on to that longing, a bit sentimental as it may be. We see in the term *shell splinter* in (2) an emphatic description of the true reality of diasporic life. Chonggi Mah of late adopts frequently an emphatic manner of speech as this, and here, too, he enounces in a high tone "I cannot deny what is meant by a shell splinter." Why is a diasporic life a shell splinter. The reason is that there's neither a sound nor a thing to be exploded or set afire. It is a world of turmoil he, a doctor in profession, and an everyday man, does not need to run into. Therefore, what he calls in this work "the abysmal life for one's free as he can no longer make a sound, nor be blown up or set afire, so free he cannot be beautiful" is a lament on a life that cannot be beautiful; this extends to realization of self that is made of shell splinters. So then what is a beautiful life? The third poem entitled "Everyday Foreign Country" consists of four parts—Spring, Summer, Fall, Winter, whose consistent tenor is longing for the land of his nativity. What causes him to stay awake in a high-class bed whereas a nap in a flat bench is a spontaneous thing is his own thought that a diasporic life is always a mere shell splinter, although he's been living abroad over ten years. It's also caused by the life there, which he deems cannot be beautiful.

Yet, surprisingly, we find in (4) a sign that he does not live such inconvenient diasporic life only. When we read the part that runs "Now a doctor myself / in a ward in a foreign country / I give flowers to the patient who's leaving the hospital," we could take the cue that perhaps his feelings of isolation / incongruity in a foreign country are being eliminated to some extent, or elevated to a higher level of love. But he says again. "Invisible flowers, / I pass on my smile / of the midsummer about a decade before." Ah, are the "invisible flowers" still palpable in the eyes of the poet. Were the flowers given to the patient who's leaving the hospital therefore "my smile of the midsummer about a decade before," in other words, the love of a Korean deeply longing for his motherland.

So my flower took a long journey.
Thou bestow meaning upon all those flowers.

Blowing, falling, fructifying,
thy fragrance.

As Chonggi Mah, thus ending "Discharge from
Hospital," intends with the word "thy fragrance" to
welcome as the matrix of love his motherland, home,
friends in early youth, and kindness, we too can have
"meaning upon all those flowers" together with him.
Here we cannot but sense that his appetent longing,
seemingly delicate, doesn't stop simply as his personal
nostalgia but instead grows into a warm, loving heart
for humans on a broader horizon.

3

I want to reiterate that what vitalizes Chonggi Mah's
poetry, although he writes "I suddenly wished to be a
"robust man," is a warm loving heart, rather than
grand manly volition. This very loving heart saddens
the solid vocational technician as a doctor, and his
comfortable diasporic life in America. This
simultaneously functions as a leverage to take him out
of established, personal category of being a doctor in
America, then to elevate to public category of a poet
who speaks a man's truth. His love, for that reason, is
magnified. Whence could his love gain such strength.
Earlier he's written a poem that reads:

When I pass by the public cemetery
it always smells of mint.
A square window smelling of mint,
the dawn outside that window
needs to practice to see the inside.
No ceiling, no floor, no corner,
the phenomenon of ionization of an individual.
I shall again set my eyes
on that vivid body raised in the night;
I'll sometime wash my hands deep
to find your fingerprint.

This is the last part of the work entitled "Instance ·
5," and earlier in the poem's beginning he confesses
the doctor's misdiagnosis and the patient's death, a
rendezvous with the dead in a dream, etc. It would be
difficult for us to deny that to this poet, who started
out all but simultaneously through medical
experience and encounter with his poetic self, his
direct / indirect acquaintance with carcasses deepened
this poet's inner world, leading him to fathom what is
meant by love's quality. When he said "the dawn
outside that window / needs to practice to see the
inside," and then "I'll sometime wash my hands deep
/ to find your fingerprint," we cannot but easily
acknowledge that he already is choosing a hard and
long road to eternal human nature, beyond each
specific physical death.

Of course, there's also a preceding evidence that much ghastlier 6 · 25 experience awakened in him the importance and difficulty of love.

> The site of Gyunghakwon, when we returned from a few years' refuge. Thin pine trees were as before and it was a bit cold and frightening, I walking alone the snowy night chose to love. Believed loving everything in the world was the only way to become a good poet.
> —midsection of "The Site of Gyunghakwon"

Dreary and ragged boyhood experiences more readily spurred him on to genial emotion of love. And that continued to grow into a love to confess love in an autopsy room, to take the reek of corpses as mint smell. The poet leaves parents and siblings to go abroad. It's an extraordinary pain for a warm loving heart to part with parents and siblings. He has nevertheless been nurturing love more and more, consistently amidst pain. It's always heartbreaking to live away from one's motherland and cherished town, apart from the beloved. Even so, he finally came to contemplate that simple longing is not love, how painful it is to be unable to do anything despite his love, and furthermore, what he ought to do when the object of his love betrays his love. That maturity we can vividly observe in the following poems.

I've taken up drawing.
Decided to be simple like winter.
The tree outside the window has fallen asleep
and images of snow
pile up inside a wanderer's bones.

I've started drawing an urn.
Decided to live like an empty field.
Let the remaining things all rot
into wine for the thirsty
and for sake of love's undergrown grass
began licking
the inward road dark and long.

The finest part in this poem "Drawing" is: "images of snow / pile up inside a wanderer's bones." Such as the scene in which Rilke, homing from wandering in the vast Russian plain, met Rodin with frazzled fingertips in his studio! We see here Chonggi Mah's love gaining a firm arm after getting around pains as best as he could. Now he knows what he longed for.

The woodwind notes playing hidden
are sweeter than love
but our classics
first let the hair down and whet a knife.

Winter night, waking up often.
Friend moaning in sleep.

INVISIBLE LAND OF LOVE

–latter part of "A Jew's Windwood Instrument"

There's a saying that goes "The farther off, the better one sees". Albeit in the distance, he's not away from us now. The poet waking up often from his sleep for a friend's moaning. It's logical at least that one can't see a far land of love, yet he begins to feel anxious for its "invisibility." The invisibility isn't something that happened yesterday, but then why so repeatedly? Here we see a small paradox that he is finally seeing something. What he's seen is a major historical circumstance which is invisible not just to himself but to all, or which all are not seeing as it is. Unlike a poet residing abroad, he is regarding that with a wider view through a profound insight into our history. A solid victory it is for the poet Chonggi Mah's love. Whether in America or in Korea, he is a poet of beautiful love, always to be with us.

This province's winds grow under the dark river,
this province's flesh and blood is where winds pull.
Outside Seosomun, the blood splashing in
    Senamteo forms a river,
dehydrated souls wake up in the river water of
    former age.
Invisible people who believe an invisible land.
–from "River in Kihae Year" in *Invisible Land of Love*

ABOUT THE AUTHOR

Chonggi Mah, the poet, was born in Tokyo, Japan, in 1939. He graduated from Yonsei University, College of Medicine, in Seoul, Korea, and subsequently attended graduate school at Seoul National University. Soon after coming to America in 1966 he was certified with the American Board of Radiology. He then worked as a professor in the Radiology Department of the Medical College of Ohio, and later as a pediatric radiologist at the Toledo Children's Hospital until his retirement in 2002.

Earlier in 1959 he made his debut as a poet through Hyundae Munhak, thereafter published *Quiet Triumph* (1960), *Second Winter* (1965), *Well-Tempered Clavier* (Anthology; Vol.1, 1968; Vol.2, 1972), *Borderland Flower* (1976), *Invisible Land of Love* (1980), *Are Reeds the Only Ones That Live Together* (1986), *Color of That Country* (1991), *Eyes of Dew* (1997), *You Can Smell Tree in Birds' Dream* (2002), and others. *Star, the Unfinished Joy* (2003) is one of his collections of essays. He has received the Korean Literary Award, the Pyunwoon Literature Award, the Yeesan Literature Award, the East-West Literature Award, among others.

Experiences as a medical doctor, remarkable as they were for a poet, and diasporic life, the greatest conflict for a poet, make up the basic motif of his poems; Ma nonetheless takes in such intense experiences to distill into beautiful, warm, and fine lyricism, by means of lucid intellect and fine-tuned language. *Invisible Land of Love* is the fruit of his poetic world striking even a fresher note in the height of his Parnassian attainment.

ABOUT THE TRANSLATOR

Youngshil Cho holds a Master of English & English Literature from Chonnam University, Korea. A recipient of numerous grants for her English translation of modern Korean literature, she has translated and published six contemporary Korean poetry books including *Paper* by Shin Dal-Ja (Codhill Press, 2018) and *Forty Two Greens* by Chonggi Mah (Codhill Press, 2020).

She has authored three books, and *Everlasting Ring* is her most recent collection of poems. "If I Become Good at Math, Could I Solve the Skies?", "Frozen Pond" and other poems written by her for young adults have appeared in some quarterly literary magazines of Korea.

www.ingramcontent.com/pod-product-compliance
Lightning Source LLC
Chambersburg PA
CBHW032105080426
42733CB00006B/432

*9 7 8 1 6 2 2 4 6 1 0 3 5 *